AIRPLANE BABY
BANANA BLANKET

By the same author

Regulator

AIRPLANE BABY BANANA BLANKET

BENJAMIN DODDS

Airplane Baby Banana Blanket
Recent Work Press
Canberra, Australia

Copyright © Benjamin Dodds, 2020

ISBN: 9780648834311(paperback)

 A catalogue record for this book is available from the National Library of Australia

All rights reserved. This book is copyright. Except for private study, research, criticism or reviews as permitted under the Copyright Act, no part of this book may be reproduced, stored in a retrieval system, or transmitted in any form by any means without prior written permission. Enquiries should be addressed to the publisher.

Cover illustrations: Caren Florence
Cover design: Recent Work Press
Set by Recent Work Press

recentworkpress.com

SS

For Lucy

Contents

1. Passengers Nod Congratulations

Norman, Oklahoma—An Early Evening in 1964	3
Good Grief, Charlie Brown	5
Jane	6
Professor Bill's Vision	8
This Woman's Work	9
The Temerlins	10
Steve	11
Heights	12
Space Chimps (i): Property of Holloman Aerospace Medical	13

2. Observer Effect

Saturday Morning	17
Running Away	19
Toilet Training	20
Discovery	21
Observer Effect	23
Intrusion	25
Sunday Drive	26
The First Bite	27
Protectress	28
Hierarchy	29
Renovations	31
Unvoiced	32
Morbid Curiosity	33
Lucy's Cat	34
Radish* and Watermelon†	36
A Little Death	38
Playgirl	39
Warm Welcome	42
The Temerlins Entertain	43
One-Off	45

Too Much of a Good Thing	46
Space Chimps (ii): Enos	48

3. American Teen

Lucy	53
A Change of Scenery	55
Captive	57
Caged	58
Stuck	59
Leaf Taker	62
Lucy Lives	64
Reunion Island	65
For a Brief and Happy While	68
Endings	69
Obituaries	71
Space Chimps (iii): Death of an Astronaut	72
The Seven Primate Ages	74

Afterword	76

Major Figures of *Airplane Baby Banana Blanket*

Dr Maurice Temerlin
Psychotherapist. Academic at the University of Oklahoma.
Jane's husband. Steve's father.

Jane Temerlin
Social worker and academic.
Maurice's wife. Steve's mother.

Steve Temerlin
Jane and Maurice's son.

Charlie Brown
The Temerlins' first chimpanzee from the University of Oklahoma's cross-fostering program.

Lucy
The Temerlins' second chimpanzee from the University of Oklahoma's cross-fostering program.

Professor William Lemmon
Chimpanzee cross-fostering pioneer.
Director of the Institute for Primate Studies at the University of Oklahoma.

Roger Fouts
Primate researcher at the University of Oklahoma.
Lucy's American Sign Language (ASL) teacher.

Janis Carter
Graduate student at the University of Oklahoma.
Initially hired to clean Lucy's living space and provide ASL practice.

Bob and Mae Noell
Owners of the roadside zoo where Lucy was born in Florida.

HAM and Enos
Chimpanzees from NASA's Project Mercury.

1.
PASSENGERS NOD
CONGRATULATIONS

Norman, Oklahoma—An Early Evening in 1964

A rich red sauce waits in a stainless bowl
set aside until Charlie Brown's bedtime.
When Jane has fed and bathed the ape
Maury our good doctor will barbecue his wife
some ribs. His sauce is basic but good:

catsup
Worcestershire
a dash of Tabasco
some garlic
lemon juice
a decent amount of honey

Their impatient early-diner climbs
into his highchair, rocks it
on inadequate legs.

Jane berates the noisemaking and stirs
a pot of oatmeal and vitamins
not expecting or prepared for
the spring-loaded leap that lands his screams
on top of the bench and unloads the bowl
all over our fourth and final player
Cocky the Moluccan cockatoo
the scene's sorry clown who's also
allowed in the kitchen of course.

She was right to erect her salmon-pink
crest in split-second anticipation
of the shitstorm's approach but too
little too late to shield her from
the sweet-smelling shadow
she'll wear like a wound
until next year's moulting.

And now here comes Jane
after a moment of absence with an air
rifle aimed and fired just above Charlie
Brown's greedy feeding
sacrificing a window
to teach a salient lesson.
Children use their manners
in the happy home
of the Temerlins.

Good Grief, Charlie Brown

Where shrieks of bedlam
are the norm, calm
pricks the ears.

It draws our good doctor
outside to a space
where chaos

can be briefly contained
if not controlled.
Pinned high

to the mesh wall of a cage
once meant to house
exotic birds

is the silence's source
tangled bundle
swaddled papoose

delivery from a hateful stork.
The chimp is dead
at the age of four—

hung out, wrung
out, suffocated
by torsion

done in by boisterous play
and the squeeze
of his own security blanket.

More Linus than Charlie Brown.

Jane

Jane is in Tampa.

Jane is in Tampa, Florida.

Jane is in Tampa, Florida, three weeks after Charlie Brown's death.

Jane is in Tampa, Florida, three weeks after Charlie Brown's death, at a roadside zoo.

Jane is in Tampa, Florida, three weeks after Charlie Brown's death, at a roadside zoo owned by Bob and Mae Noell.

Jane is in Tampa, Florida, three weeks after Charlie Brown's death, at a roadside zoo owned by Bob and Mae Noell who've been phoned by Professor Bill Lemmon.

Jane is in Tampa, Florida, three weeks after Charlie Brown's death, at a roadside zoo owned by Bob and Mae Noell who've been phoned by Professor Bill Lemmon, Jane and Maury's superior.

Jane is in Tampa, Florida, three weeks after Charlie Brown's death, at a roadside zoo owned by Bob and Mae Noell who've been phoned by Professor Bill Lemmon, Jane and Maury's superior (and their psychotherapist).

Jane is in Tampa, Florida, three weeks after Charlie Brown's death, at a roadside zoo owned by Bob and Mae Noell who've been phoned by Professor Bill Lemmon, Jane and Maury's superior (and their psychotherapist), concerning a chimpanzee.

Jane is in Tampa, Florida, three weeks after Charlie Brown's death, at a roadside zoo owned by Bob and Mae Noell who've been phoned by Professor Bill Lemmon, Jane and Maury's superior (and their psychotherapist), concerning a chimpanzee pregnant with a daughter.

Jane is in Tampa, Florida, three weeks after Charlie Brown's death, at a roadside zoo owned by Bob and Mae Noell who've been phoned by Professor Bill Lemmon, Jane and Maury's superior (and their psychotherapist), concerning a chimpanzee pregnant with a daughter she'll mother for a night.

Professor Bill's Vision

[William Lemmon] explained that [Bob and Mae Noells'] chimps would be living like kings and queens in human homes—the homes of Oklahoma University psychology professors whom Lemmon had personally chosen for this singular honor—where they would get better treatment than they would just about anywhere else.

—*Elizabeth Hess,* Nim Chimpsky

The key is
to obtain the subject
before it knows
what it is.
Early enough to avoid
the compromising risk
of its brief mother.
Timing is critical
to ensure integrity
of so unique an opportunity.
Just how chimpanzee
can *Pan troglodytes* be
when raised among us
in modern homes
or is chimp-essence
baked in at birth?
What truths can be gleaned
when we rear another's
clean slate as we do
our own?

This Woman's Work

The airplane flight and the act of taking Lucy away from her mother had been for Jane the symbolic equivalent of the act of giving birth.

—*Maurice Temerlin,* Lucy: Growing Up Human

In exchange
   for a daughter
      Jane Temerlin
         offered a Coke.
Such sweetness
   tickles the tongue
      and masks the
         phencyclidine
that allowed Bob
   and Mae Noell to pull
      from fortressed arms
         something pink
and rare.
   Somewhere above Alabama
      passengers nod
         congratulations
to a mother
   tending a covered
      bassinet, hushing
         gentle reassurance
to a child she calls
   Lucy.

The Temerlins

Eclectic sleep-sounds
fill the home of the Temerlins.
Tonight's ragged snore
of a teaching psycho-
therapist does not disturb
his travel-wearied
social worker wife.
Neither hears the tiny
rhythmic breaths
of a two-day-old chimp
at the edge of their bed.
Before lights out
they noted sharp pleasure
at wheeling the crib in again—
years since Steve was a boy.

Steve

Steve keeps her
at arms' length.
He won't involve

himself in the tiny life
of another one.
She's even more

fragile than Charlie
who'd arrived
at the age of three

and turned out
to be quite
fragile enough.

It's too soon
for replacement
siblings when

he still misses
the first so much.
Yet he warms

to her within a day
allows clinging cuddles
shoulder rides

the wet way she covers
his entire mouth
with her own.

Heights

Steve steadies
the fourteen-month-old
in the fork
of a backyard mimosa's
very lowest branch.
She's terrified
and cries
for her brother
to unhand her
to give back the safety
of lawn's green low.
He isn't cruel.
The pre-teen
lets her down and tries
again with another tree
another branch
even lower than the last.
Longterm investment
of brotherly play
will one day yield
the wisdom
that windblown canopies
are perfect
hiding places in times
of mischief
when our good doctor
and his wife
call out her name
but for now Lucy has had
quite enough. She knocks
at the door
waits to be let back inside.

Space Chimps (i)
Property of Holloman Aerospace Medical

The
sub-orbital
deed poll of a
job well done lets
Subject 65 splash down
in the Atlantic with a new, more
TV-friendly name. HAM—acronym
for the place he was trained—rides the
swell in the damaged, leaky capsule that topped
his very own Redstone rocket at launch twenty minutes ago.
First came crushing G force, far greater than anyone planned
then brief relief of weightlessness before downward slide along an
equal and opposite parabola arm sleeved in coruscating flame and the
strange and furious scent of burning toast. They arrive to raise his sinking sieve and

photographers flash his massive grin around the globe. He's got The Right Stuff, this guy.

The newspapers cite his smile as proof: *All in a day's work*, says his padlocked rockstar-
rictus, framed on all sides by an inch-wide border of gum. Is it helpful
to know that true chimp contentment is lip-sheathed, relaxed and
mouth-hidden, or that Goodall caught HAM's frenzied press
and dubbed him the world's most terrified chimp?
Brave and happy primate, astronaut native

of Cameroon, first ape to cross the
threshold of space (ten whole
weeks before Gagarin)
the good people of

planet Earth
salute
you.

2.
OBSERVER EFFECT

Saturday Morning

Jane has learned
to take the middle road

when wheeling Lucy
down supermarket aisles.

Bottles, jars and boxes
are equidistantly off-limits

to the black-downed octopus-arms
that never fail to seize

their chance to reach and claim
such prizes, to bring them

curling brightly into soft, open
mouth for further appraisal.

Today they are all together.
Why not turn tedious chore

into an hour of family time?
A man in a tie meets them

by the cereal, excuses
himself in a humourless way

lets them know there's been
a complaint, that pets

aren't allowed in the store.
Our good doctor pins him in place

with steady eyes
counters disrespect

with explanation
concise as it is true:

She's our daughter.

Gently parted lips and low laughing
huffs confirm the girl's approval.

She reaches for a Temerlin
hand. Any will do.

Running Away

In a patchy clearing
   half a mile from home
      Lucy lies waiting in weed—
         the latest favourite game.

She knows what keys are for
   and that every Temerlin door
      (inside and out) can be opened
         without a great deal of fuss.

Smooth rotation of the stolen
   brass shard she turns over
      now in her mouth is really all
         it takes. She twirls grass ribbon

around long fingers and pulls
   until satisfying tear and snap
      give up sharp wafts of green.
         Or, she has found, if she grips

lower down, a sudden
   heavy harvest of soil
      hangs in momentary cloud
         there for a beat and then gone

riding the same breeze
   that brings afternoon sounds
      of children, distant dogs and
         the incessant call of her name.

Toilet Training

Maurice likes to find faeces
in its appropriate place.

The green shag rug beneath
the glass coffee table is
not deemed acceptable

yet his daughter favours
the spot over any other.
They've taken to leaving doors
wide open when using the bathroom

in the hopeful spirit of *monkey see
monkey do* (and yes they know
a chimp's not a monkey) but
even when she does climb up

to leave a token turd in the bowl
she never fails to cut it short
in order to save some

for the glass-lidded nest
at the family room's core.

Discovery

(i)

At the family-room rug's edge
she juggles pliers and a mirror
    deft and skilful use of household tools.

It took time to master the double-armed
first order lever but she managed and even
    added her own clever level of simian complexity—

harsh jaws flipped and treated as handles ensure a safe
and rubber-soft means of entry as she lowers
    herself over Jane's unclasped compact.

She opens dull arms when they find their tender mark
and looks through the glass circle to a parted pair of
    labia, new and inexhaustible source of fascination.

(ii)

A sharpened pencil's
    glancing weight

gives soft and precise satisfaction
    when led in concert with sure

slender fingers around and about
    the limits of her lazy opening.

She lies prone on the couch
    alongside our good doctor

notices now that his book hangs
    forgotten around a thumb

as he watches her quiet
    absent-minded play.

Everything is sudden boredom to her.
    She leaves in search of something new.

He contemplates the pencil she's gifted him
    far less scandalised

than the layman might be.

Observer Effect

How to capture it
        on film
if she won't continue
            with a camera
in the room?
        The family sees it daily
constantly finds her
            in flagrante delicto
(good luck trying to ignore
               the noisy business)
but everything stops in its tracks
                 if anyone
plays photographer.
            Psychology Today needs pictures
if they're to make much
            of our good doctor's reports.
He has shots
        of the concertinaed hose
held at arms' length
            in elongated hands
and others that show the way she
                grooms coarse-haired limbs
with rattling suction.
            They have captured the times
she reverses its flow
            to let the machine
breathe dust down her throat
               but never have they documented
the sucking stream
            of the vacuum cleaner
as it pulls at what it finds
                between chimpanzee legs
bringing giggling
        release.

Maurice Temerlin, PhD
        knows the observer effect's
problematic skew.
        He teaches it to
undergrads.
    Christ almighty
here it is
    in his own home.

Intrusion

Shaken awake by his wife
he slides from the covers
cocks his pistol

moves in deep and silent
crouch toward the family room
and queer racket beyond

stands naked in black kitchen
sends out bloodless fingers
for elusive enlightenment

slaps at electric revelation
when a steady hand closes
expertly around an ankle

She shrinks back
in scream-white glare

the cupboards' wide-flung arms

the Kelvinator's
mothering hum

Sunday Drive

She will not be touched
in the car. Jane's hand on her
knee, Steve's leaning shoulder
our good doctor's trimmed nails
resting on her scalp—all firmly
rejected when they're out and on
the road. It makes sense, really.
Vigilance and all eyes ahead.
No place for anytime-affection
when flying at terrible speeds.
Her steadfast rule's exception
is fast approaching now.
She feels its presence far in advance
mixture of water, height and sound.
A few miles out from the weekend ranch
they'll slow to hump over warped
and sun-scraped planks
as she begins to climb torsos
embrace with her whole
self the fronts of heads
bounce, pinch, pull
and dig into the ones she loves.
How tightly need a chimpanzee squeeze
how much louder can she whine
to cut through family madness
to shock them all from calm?
Why does nobody share
her screaming fear of bridges?

The First Bite

(i)

A game with the girl
gets as rough as they'll let it.
She needs to know limits
seeks equal resistance
to her effortless strength. Reparation
for a stinging fistful of Jane's long braid
comes fast and free in the glossy black
form of a forearm held easily in reach.
She pushes to be pushed back, wrestles
to be enveloped in return, craves boundary's
attentive embrace. Maurice is not surprised
in the least when his daughter
bites Rose on the hand.

(ii)

Rose is a regular at therapy
sessions. A circle of six or seven
housewives arranged on the family
room's floor. Nothing off-limits, all
thoughts heard and heeded in earnest.
She'll be bitten soon enough, but first
the latest serving of distant husband
and the son who won't come down
from the roof. Maury will later admit
to doubts, but lets the lady stay back
to meet and play with
his rambunctious girl.

Protectress

In nature no chimpanzee knows his own father, either in the biological sense of the male who impregnated his mother, or in the social sense of the male as a protector.

—Dr Maurice K. Temerlin, Psychology Today,
  November, 1975

In early days, Lucy
was indifferent to sex.
Jane and Maury fucked
unmolested as she lay
in infant sleep beside
their bucking bed, but since
the age of two-and-a-bit
she hasn't missed a thing.
As in the wild, maternal cries
raise alarm in the child;
it's up to the daughter
to deliver poor Jane
from harm. She somersaults
onto the mattress, knocks
a full glass to the floor
tries to distract with grunts
of her own, but she knows
it'll take something more.
The bed's a blur of beast
all hair, all fists, all teeth
no time to guess
where her father has gone
as she drags this thing
out of her mother.

Hierarchy

Scientist soldier
she is diligent student of rank

Lowest are strangers
   home-world intruders
      nothing to her

Next, acquaintances
   (graduate strangers)
      patient investors of time

Family claims the rarest
   air at the pyramid's highest steps
      brother Steve
         just below father Maurice

but each must raise eyes
   to meet Jane's benevolent gaze
      the girl's live-in queen
         mother of all she surveys

In every interaction, Lucy calculates, chooses sides

brother and classmate
   wrestle a sun-faded football—
      kid takes home
         teethmarks in his thigh

Son whines at father
   over unfair chores—
      swaying stare and threatening bark
         ensure soapy dishes are rinsed and dried

    Jane and Maury raise voices
       over a colleague's recent paper—
         hackles and gums on show
           she backs
                herself into mother's perfect lap

Renovations

Lucky Lucy is big enough now
for her very own grown-up bedroom.
At some expense, the Temerlin place
is being greatly altered
and soon the Oklahoma home
will boast a new extension
the grandest of cages.
It takes sturdy stuff
to house a rapidly ripening
female ape. An adolescent
tantrum's rage can kick down
concrete unless heavy gauge
steel reinforcement is threaded
completely throughout. Maurice is keen
for the project's completion
a space for his daughter
to be herself
a Woolfian
room of her own.

Unvoiced

Before visits most days, she's ready—poised
to wrap an OU grad in long strong arms.
She shows Roger or Janis or Sue to the kitchen
(two happy mugs on the table, kettle on the boil)
climbs from counter to cabinet, finds tea in its tin.
They sit and sip together until the lesson begins.
Positioning her hands in brand new ways
showing how to hold fingers in just the right
shape by doing the same with their own
manual choreography christens her world.
She gathers in glad handfuls the fresh
vocab they bring. Curriculum today
is swallowed whole. She knows signs
for *orange* and *candy,* can show that
both are *sweet,* both *food,* but now
comes sharper knowledge that
only one is *fruit.* At hour's end
the visitor will rise and leave.
She presses her face against
windows with driveway
views, leans heavily
waves the good
friend goodbye
until someone
yells *Get
down.*

Morbid Curiosity

The armadillo's carapace
lifts away easily as pork

crackling from Sunday evening's
roast. It's been here a while.

She caught vague notes
of decay when last they came

to the family ranch, but today
come brazen front-row chords

of advanced decomposition.
Lucy lifts it by a back leg

hangnail-husk flaps back
to let insides out.

Incoming voices bark
for her to drop it

but the carcass falls
of its own accord

denying the chance
to defy or comply.

She chooses
to carry the foot

in her fist for the rest
of the afternoon.

Lucy's Cat

(i)

*Put the damned thing
down and let it walk.*
She lowers the tabby
almost to the floor
skims hovering paws
just above carpet.
Told again to *let-it-go!*
she does, but cups
huge hands into a corral
that tracks it inescapably left
right, forward, back.
She can't handle not holding
the thing's small warmth
for as long as this and swoops
it onto juggling shoulders where
needle claws bite deep.

(ii)

Teacher grips tiny student
in tightly fisted foot, stills
its thrashing head patiently
to aim at new knowledge. *Book*
she signs in her best ASL—
two blue-black palms hinge apart
lengthwise to ape a spread of pages.
Before the pupil's flinching face
an open paperback waves wildly
held between the dextrous toes
of Miss Lucy's other foot.

(iii)

For a brief unmonitored moment
the litter tray is glad sanctuary
scat-strewn paradise of peace.
But chimp finds cat again
and flies down the hall
to suspend it over the bowl.
Kong wants Fay Wray
to shit like a lady.

Radish* and Watermelon†

Roger was teaching her one sign at a time, then observing any generalisation which might occur to new situations.

—Maurice Temerlin, Lucy: Growing Up Human

airplane baby
banana blanket
book
candy
can't car cat
catch
come-gimme
cry dirty drink
eat enough food
fruit go grass hug
hurry hurt
Jane
Janis key
kiss
leash
listen look
Lucy Maury
me
mine mirror more
no open
orange
paper please
radio
*hurt-cry-food
Roger
run
smell smile sorry Steve

Sue swallow tea
tickle want
†candy-fruit
yes

A Little Death

Maury hauls himself
into her roof-top room

    finds crouched blackness
backed against bone-white wall

    and a caramel corpse
in the corner. He's never seen

his girl like this.
Squeals that drew him here

since-ceased, she hangs
in freeze-frame
    complete with celluloid tremble

won't look away
when he raises nearly nothing

in the hollow of his hands.
Button-hole mouth is free

of blood, frail frame remains
unbroken—things look and feel

just as they should.
She doesn't exhale

until he takes
the cat away.

Playgirl

When in full estrus, an erotic response may be elicited by a photograph of a nude male.

—Maurice Temerlin, Lucy: Growing Up Human

He wants to elicit
erotic response
in his sometimes-subject
daughter. This week's
Cosmo provides a burly Burt
Reynolds reclining atop
a bear-skin. He's naked enough
but a hand hides his cock
so our good doctor purchases
Playgirl. Plenty of penises
freely on show. None are erect
but beggars can't choose.

She's in heat
on a towel
on the sofa
a cool and clear drink
in her hand.
Jane has one, too.
They turn tipsy
gin-and-tonic heads
at the key-drop coming
of father and husband
Maurice.

For Lucy, he says
drops the gloss-heavy thing
in the girl's lazy lap. She's fluent

in pictures, hunts them in papers
and Golden Books, but isn't
impressed by these housewives
in heels selling slim cigarettes.
Then she discovers the men.

The whimper she makes
is at first quite familiar
they've heard favourite foods
bring the same, but soft happy
huffs build up to a grunt
as she moves the show
down to the floor.
She pinches at
nakedness
gently at first
rubs the pads
of her fingers
across youthful groins.
Each new member adds
urgency, pawing finds purchase
in whitening scratch, thick nails
abrade and pierce paper.
Frenzied friction
claims prick
after prick.

The wild chimpanzee
in the family room
crouches and bounces
in florid squat, kisses wet sex
to each defaced page.
Manhood missing
scraped away in excitement
she straddles the centrepiece
centrefold's wide-flung wings
and performs a slick trick

of disappearing digits.
A shuddering
hoot and the magazine's
pulped in a perfectly aimed
jet of piss.

Lucy Temerlin leaves
her folks in wide-eyed quiet
to measure
three fingers
of gin.

Warm Welcome

Two hours of slow sliding on icy
night roads more than earn a generous
colleague his pitstop on return
from an interstate conference. Our good
doctor, thankful for the lift, is home now
and not far from sleep, but George
still has miles and an urgent need to pee.
Shown down a dark hall to the bathroom, he
slips in, leaves the door just ajar. In bare bulb's
glare, he hangs back his head and unzips
to unleash sighing relief. The pair
are unacquainted, but late-night Lucy's
here to play and, by George, she'll be
damned if a guest goes ungreeted. They meet
midstream—her flip-top face split at the jaw.
Four incisors frame a wine-glass throat
that swills and swallows sparkling froth.
The chaos and din are standard
but her prize tonight is new.
Spit-thickened swish
of newcomer's piss runs
warm between chimp-cheek
and gum.

The Temerlins Entertain

Adorable,
just adorable—

the chairman's wife's words
don't match her eyes.

The seated creature's
leathered palm floats
unreceived, unshaken
over straightened fork
and knife.

Lady guest and husband
cradle glasses like life-support
as their hosts push small-talk
uphill.

A whiskey sour touches
table for an instant—
time enough for swift theft
to occur. The thing
is thirsty

pours stolen cocktail
down open throat
maraschino
and all.

The dribble saved
and set back on
cork coaster
fails to impress.

It knows its place
sees it's gone too far
leaps to the bar for fresh drinks
serves company before itself.

One-Off

She has never met
another Does not know

they can exist
Is unaware

she's one herself
Expecting

a spark they bring it into her
space Male sexually mature

Outstretched hand puzzles
confuses appals Alert amber

eyes penetrate her own
uninvited *Get it out Get It*

Out she shrieks in sound
and sign Afraid

of mirror monsters she lays
it on extra thick Wild

enough for them to
abort the thing

completely

Too Much of a Good Thing

I hate books which have no ending—like this one. The story of Lucy Temerlin is not finished. Jane and Steve and I talk constantly about it, but it is very complicated, for we want to live normal lives now, though we are still committed to Lucy.

—*Maurice Temerlin,* Lucy: Growing Up Human

The book is almost done, though academia
has largely turned its back. She's a human

interest piece at most, her experimental
existence too sideshow for establishment, too

folksy for worthier journals, too tainted by
scientist love. Her biography covers too much

of the personal, far too much of her privates.
Science doesn't favour the fringe, won't entertain

the anecdotal. Into double digits now, stronger
than her family combined, she is heavyweight

cramper of style. A recent unencumbered trip
to San Francisco was the first our good doctor

and wife had shared since 1964, decade-lost
joy afforded only by rare visit from son Steve

dearly missed brother who stayed and played
with his sister for the week, just like

the good old days. Is this how the other half
lives—free from fear of unpredictability

heedless of animal whim? Stroll the Golden
Gate today, cruise Alcatraz tomorrow.

Daughter's manifold needs
begin to exceed family means.

All Temerlin futures look Lucyless.

Space Chimps (ii)
Enos

Remember your training, man.
Three discrete shapes on a screen:
circle, triangle, circle. The eggheads
call it an 'oddity problem'—find the anomaly
give its lever a pull. Nicely done.
From a chute your pellet
of freeze-dried fruit drops: reward.

Up for another? Two green triangles
a solitary circle. Can't fool this one
boys! He's here to impress.
Just as in ground-training
chimp Enos, crewman-simulate
NASA's puzzle champ, doesn't miss
a trick. Forget that every
hour-and-a-half he racks
up another loop of the earth.

He aims for perfect score
banana pellets on-tap—not once today
(the day that counts)
has our guy been dealt the zap
—screwing the soles of two
wrinkly feet to live electrodes
was someone's pre-launch
waste of time. The next geometric
trio's just as preschool-easy.
He slaps at the answer
not skipping a beat

      but searing voltage
              pierces feet as he transmits
      a stream of squealing telemetry down to Mission
Control. Something's
            not right, but the fault doesn't lie
with him.
      The next response (correct, of course)
earns a jolt that would   bounce him
         out of his   seat if only the   straps
     offered slack.

With each fresh orbit, Enos
isolates, indicates
anomalous shapes, waits
for food and the hard-earned
relief that long ago ceased
to come. Someone'll
have to write this all up.
Why does nothing
work as it should?

3.
AMERICAN TEEN

Lucy

Lucy flies.

Lucy flies over the Atlantic.

Lucy flies over the Atlantic with her parents.

Lucy flies over the Atlantic with her parents and their paid academic friend.

Lucy flies over the Atlantic with her parents and their paid academic friend on her way to Abuko Reserve.

Lucy flies over the Atlantic with her parents and their paid academic friend on her way to Abuko Reserve in the Gambia.

Lucy flies over the Atlantic with her parents and their paid academic friend on her way to Abuko Reserve in the Gambia (instead of a zoo).

Lucy flies over the Atlantic with her parents and their paid academic friend on her way to Abuko Reserve in the Gambia (instead of a zoo or a medical lab).

Lucy flies over the Atlantic with her parents and their paid academic friend on her way to Abuko Reserve in the Gambia (instead of a zoo or a medical lab, two other considered options).

Lucy flies over the Atlantic with her parents and their paid academic friend on her way to Abuko Reserve in the Gambia (instead of a zoo or a medical lab, two other considered options), not yet knowing she's left her childhood home.

Lucy flies over the Atlantic with her parents and their paid academic friend on her way to Abuko Reserve in the Gambia (instead of a zoo or a medical lab, two other considered options), not yet knowing she's left her childhood home and life behind for good.

Lucy flies over the Atlantic with her parents and their paid academic friend on her way to Abuko Reserve in the Gambia (instead of a zoo or a medical lab, two other considered options), not yet knowing she's left her childhood home and life behind for good as she's drugged with phencyclidine.

Lucy flies over the Atlantic with her parents and their paid academic friend on her way to Abuko Reserve in the Gambia (instead of a zoo or a medical lab, two other considered options), not yet knowing she's left her childhood home and life behind for good as she's drugged with phencyclidine, sealed inside a crate.

A Change of Scenery

"At the end of those three weeks, there was just no way that I could leave Lucy."

—*Janis Carter,* RadioLab

In their animal way
they scare her
    these others by the cageful
        enclosed in enclosures
            steeped in Gambian heat.
She met one only once
    conspirator-intruder
    into her Oklahoma home
        worked her hardest since
            to forget the inhuman thing.
They're everywhere here
    outside   her head
    and in.
And no hint of Jane or Maurice
for weeks
    just Janis, the one
    who sometimes signs
    as she cleans
    and plays learning games
    back at home.
        Strange to see her
        for this long.
Even more's new
in this odd normal
    enough to fill up
        three pestilential years—

       slow acceptance of
       gnat and mosquito itch
          acquaintance with
          skin infection's
          flake
                steady hair and
                weight loss
                      transition
                      to transfusions.
She knows she's not alone
    hasn't stopped to consider
    just how she understands
        that these chatterers
        complain of the
        same.

Captive

The woman wakes
into caged night
perhaps disturbed
by lightning. Low
waves of thunder confirm
her drowsy hunch from
across the Gambia's slow
flow on both of the slender
island's sides.
She senses them
immediately, their close fear
of storm, a nest of gathered unease
above her makeshift bed. Hanging
bodies compress the humid space
that holds them at arms' length. She can't see
but knows eager fingers search through the ceiling
mesh they've made their nightly hammock
mocking any human separation she'd planned.
They crave her even during sleep
rescuer from Abuko's stagnant refuge
hailed saviour from years of disease.
From one, surely Lucy, a whimper
dares not challenge the dark.
Strobed flash again
white jungle, before scattered splash
on swept earth floor, wet
warmth against her face, sour
taste of animal rain.

Caged

A friendly British army unit on manoeuvres had taken pity on Carter and constructed a cage on the island, not for the chimps, but for her.

—Chicago Tribune, *November 26, 1986*

inside are
blankets
    outside
      jungle
inside
cups and bottles
    outside
      the tan river
inside is
an armchair
    outside
      bare earth
inside
gin and coffee
    outside are
      insects
inside is
food
    outside
      roots and berries
inside
radio mumble
    outside
      birds
inside is
Janis Carter
    outside are
      eight chimpanzees, the island and Lucy

Stuck

"You're sitting here now, at a table. And she sat at a table [...] How would it be to take all your clothes off and go out into that tree?"

—Mae Noell, interview in Visions of Caliban

They are chimpanzees again
these eight erstwhile
dwellers among men—solitary
performers, pets, bootleg
menagerie tenants.
A long year's green key
unbarred memory
of animal past, whispered
to them what they were, aired
out human habit. They rattle now
round 300 man-empty jungle acres
remembering as they forget.
No such luck
for fellow number 9.
Oklahoman by way
of Florida, she never lost
what they've regained.
Their African reward is her
punishment and as they go
wild with recollection's
revelation, she clings
to the outside of Carter's
cage—wallflower
of Baboon Island.
What worked well
for the others
fails for Lucy.
The woman makes

great show of climbing
into trees, pointing out green
figs and branch-crawling ants.
She knows the diet of *Pan
troglodytes* first hand
has made herself cramp
with countless shades
of unripeness, trusting
in *monkey see
monkey do* (and yes
she knows a chimp's
not a monkey). See
the others, Lucy? Watch
how they pull themselves up
into fruit-laden canopies. Here
another route. Use this easier
climb to match their height
then swing across. Won't
follow them? At least watch
me. Here, like this. See all
the fruit? Catch, it's good.
The American teen
at the baobab's base
looks up with full mouth
signs *more food*.
Janis get. Drinking's
the same. She wants
cup and glass, gin
if she can get it
not the flat river lap
at the island's skirt.
She shuns hippo
humph and muddy feet
in favour of dented canteen.
On days meant as
weaning isolation, she
beams ASL through bars

at a blankly turned back.
food. drink. Janis. come out.
The rationed response
is *no. Lucy. go.* and
the turning away starts
again. *no. Janis. come.*
Janis. come out.
Lucy. hurt.

Leaf Taker

The thinnest
islander
by far
starves
except
when fed
by family
friend. She
will not fend
for herself
will not feed
on found food
only takes
what's given.
The giver
who so
rarely gives
of late
sits away
by the river
moves to keep
distance when
the islander
arrives on
gritty
beach.
As giver
friend
failure
she buries
herself
in grass
wrung out
strung out

alone
asleep.
Awake
to a leaf
held out
by a hand
that trembles
with hunger.
Friend
chews a
bitter bite
for show
offers to
share
the gift
    but
islander
declines
shocks
snaps off
her own fresh
green.
It tastes like
the rest of
her days.

Lucy Lives

Fact facer, wall-writing
reader, waker and smeller
of early morning coffee
our girl got there
in the end. Lucy
has learned to look
after herself. And not
one moment
too soon. Janis
provider-protector
has vanished
from Baboon Island
is banished
from Baboon Island
deposed, attacked
by a male known as
Dash. She'd be dead
but for shirt-snagging
bramble as he dragged her
through jungle, slimmest
of chances to roll
into rescuing river.
Lucy Temerlin lives
as chimpanzee, alone
with the others, couldn't
beat them, so joined them
apes their alien
ways, far
as they are
from how
she was raised.

Reunion Island

The narrow boat seats three.
Its ancient outboard fights

through sepia waters.
The driver beaches

in slushy sand
as the woman in the bow

steps down to stand
in ankle-lapping river.

From a screen of trees
comes screamed greeting.

It's been a long while.
Group of nine jostles, pants

sways its way
to meet a familiar face.

They reach to touch her
with leathered fingers

rise up to her height
to pull at her hair, circle

and dance and shake
her shoulders. She is

not afraid as she knows
their ways, understands

that they mean no harm.
Their space invasion is hail

and welcome.
One, though, sits away

awaiting a break in events
holding off until it can have her

whole. And when time
comes, when the rest

grow weary of salutation
it leans in, breathes quiet love

takes both of her hands
in its own.

There is a photograph
taken from the boat—

Carter and Temerlin
sit together in sand

embrace preserved in
monochrome. Chimp brow

rests against woman's breast
black tressed arms encircle

completely. The human's
grip is just as tight.

The image, of course
is silent. Carter carries gifts

in a cream canvas bag
mirror, brush and book

forgotten treasures
laid now in animal hands.

Weight and shape
wake something

fleeting homefires spark
but Lucy takes the bag

stows knick-knacks
back inside, returns

it all to the woman
on her beach.

Forehead
to forehead

wet pout and
one final squeeze

nine chimps
climb into their island.

For a Brief and Happy While

the motherless child
   has a son.
For now
   his clinging bird-weight
      is never far
         from her waist's
            black saddle.
She gathered
   him up
      soon after
         the death
let the lost thing ride out
   its pink grief.
They nest high
   together
      through bright
         star-sieved night
         blessed rest
            after long needful days.

Endings

(i)

She has not been
seen for weeks until
today, not that they've
been looking. New green
rises through her wide
scattering. Leaves layer
as they land. There are signs
of animal intervention, opportune
hyenas, pragmatic pigs picking
apart what she was. Given these
(and wet-season's heavy heat
industrious insects, keen interest
from carrion birds), her missing
extremities and mostly stripped
skin are unsurprising.
A mature male, trouble-maker
claims the old campsite as his own.
The reserve's rangers know
he can't be far off, so no time
for thorough searching
around Carter's abandoned cage
to find Lucy in her fullness
just hasty collection
of what lies about—
a gap-toothed girl-chimp
in parts and pieces, bones
of an almost-body
bundled into hessian.

(ii)

Who killed Lucy Temerlin?
'Twas I, said the poacher.
I ambushed the girl.
I macheted her hands and feet
for blackmarket trophies.
No, I, said the jealous islander
one of her kind. It was I who ended
her sorry life in red, unstoppable rage.
I shot poor Lucy, said the fisherman.
She caught us off-guard
surprised my men
with bold familiarity.
It was I, said the summer storm.
A single white strike.
No, I am the villain
the crocodile said.
I stalked her at the water's edge
and chewed her to pieces.
It was I, said disease. I felled her
in one humid week.
You all lie, said the venomous snake.
I struck as she traipsed
through my hissing grass.
I ended Lucy Temerlin's life
said the fat baobab. She fell hard
from my cradling branches.

Obituaries

Dead
 of a weak heart
 aged 64
  skiing somewhere
  in Oregon
  in 1988
  Found
   partially skeletonised
   aged 23
   without hands or feet
  on Baboon Island
 in 1987
 Scientist
  Subject
   Father
    Daughter
     Husband
      Sister
       Grandfather
        Mother
         Therapist
          Excommunicate
          Our good doctor
         Chimpanzee
         Maurice
        Lucy
        Temerlin

Space Chimps (iii)
Death of an Astronaut

Where lies Enos (Hebrew for Man)?

    Not mouldering beside
the deboned body-glove of
HAM's formless flesh

underneath a New
Mexico museum's
carpark flagpole

    nor laid out
in the airforce
pathology lab's
specimen drawers

that house the same's beetle-
scrubbed bones.

When half-hearted dissectors
   were done with Enos
   first chimpanzee
   to gain true orbit

(third
hominid
after two
cosmonauts)

their flayed pilot
bloomed
in flame

   not on thrilling
  re-entry but in
  medical incinerator.

Nothing of him remains.
  No brass plaque
  or ash-scattered
  park claims
  space for Enos
   (Hebrew for Man).

The Seven Primate Ages

Infant
Milk-skinned jelly of vulnerability
barely set, held against swollen
breast of all-providing goddess
take of her warmth, food, protection
mobility. She lives for you.

Juvenile
Learn through mimicry's green
games, ape the actions of those who
teach you still. Watch their ways
as you play the fool. Live well
the age of the student clown.

Adolescent
Bodies carry pleasure. This you
come to know through creative
means, scratching insistent itches. Soon
by new and richly thickened existence
know that sex's exultation is not
halved when shared.

New Parent
Curb playful fervour, put second
the self. You are needed now. Keep
safe and sated the helpless thing that craves
your scent. Shepherd small beginnings:
the rest for you is cream.

Experienced Parent
They are yours, almost
ready for their own. Others
know your quiet
success, count you gladly
in their number.

Wise Elder
From treetops, keep order.
Step down amongst those who
dwell in dispute, model ways
that were modelled for you. Parcel
out peace to your troop.

Declining Elder
Few rove so far this way.
Fortune swept your path
of accident, violence, disease.
Rest now, worry not—
let predators come.

Afterword

This book interprets another—a true story bizarre, fascinating and unsettling in fairly equal parts—Dr Maurice Temerlin's *Lucy: Growing Up Human*. Long out of print, Temerlin's unique memoir chronicles the years during which Lucy, a chimpanzee, lived with the author, his wife and his son as another member of their Oklahoma family. Maury Temerlin's 1975 text regularly refers to Lucy as his daughter, but as I devoured his supremely odd book, it became awfully clear to me that she was also his scientific subject. My collection of Lucy-themed poetry grew out of tales of the fraught hybrid life of a chimp/human/daughter/specimen.

The opening two sections of *Airplane Baby Banana Blanket* were written in direct response to events and themes from *Lucy: Growing Up Human*, which Temerlin purported to be an accurate account of Lucy's first 13 years of life. His text ends with an air of uncertainty—beyond the walls of the family home, Lucy's future was not yet decided. My poems addressing her later difficult time in the Gambia stem not from memoir, but from various articles, interviews, book chapters and podcast episodes (namely, the excellent *Radiolab* where I first chanced upon Lucy and the Temerlins). In the occasional gap I found in Lucy's story, such as an incomplete timeline or conflicting accounts, I employed bridging imagination.

Though *Airplane Baby Banana Blanket* is inspired by and closely based upon actual individuals and events, all thoughts, feelings and positions conveyed by these poems come entirely from my own mind. Other than direct quotations in epigraphs, the statements and opinions of all historical figures represented within this collection are the product of pure poetic license.

Though I have been affected deeply by my encounter with Lucy Temerlin's story, this collection is, of course, only one possible artistic interpretation of her biography. Readers may be inspired to seek out her 'father's' original text, if only to verify some of the more extreme goings-on at the Temerlin residence, remembering all the while that even our 'good doctor's' account of the chimp's extraordinary life is a second-hand one—nobody will ever read Lucy's *auto*biography.

Notes

Unless otherwise stated, all of the poems in the first two sections of *Airplane Baby Banana Blanket* are based on events in Maurice Temerlin's memoir *Lucy: Growing Up Human: A Chimpanzee Daughter in a Psychotherapist's Family* (Science & Behavior Books Inc., 1975).

'Good Grief, Charlie Brown' makes reference to characters from the *Peanuts©* comic strips by Charles M. Schultz.

'Professor Bill's Vision' contains an epigraph from Elizabeth Hess's *Nim Chimpsky: The Chimp Who Would Be Human* (Bantam, 2009).

'This Woman's Work' takes its title from a Kate Bush song of the same name from her album *The Sensual World* (EMI, 1989).

'Space Chimps (i): Property of Holloman Aerospace Medical' is based on factual information from Colin Burgess and Chris Dubbs's *Animals in Space: From Research Rockets to the Space Shuttle* (Praxis, 2007) and Dallas Campbell's *Ad Astra: An Illustrated Guide to Leaving the Planet* (Simon & Schuster, 2017).

'Protectress' contains an epigraph from Dr Maurice K. Temerlin's article in the November, 1975 issue of *Psychology Today*.

'Radish* and Watermelon†' contains a selection of Lucy's repertoire of American Sign Language vocabulary as listed in a table in Maurice Temerlin's *Lucy: Growing Up Human: A Chimpanzee Daughter in a Psychotherapist's Family* (Science & Behavior Books Inc., 1975).

'One-Off', 'Lucy', 'A Change of Scenery', 'Captive', 'Caged', 'Stuck', 'Leaf Taker', 'Lucy Lives' and 'Reunion Island' are all based on events detailed in the 'Lucy' episode of the *Radiolab* podcast (WNYC, 2010).

'Space Chimps (ii): Enos' is based on factual information from the report *Results of the Project Mercury Ballistic and Orbital Chimpanzee Flights*

(NASA, 1963) and from Colin Burgess and Chris Dubbs's *Animals in Space: From Research Rockets to the Space Shuttle* (Praxis, 2007).

'Caged' contains an epigraph from the newspaper article 'Going Ape in the Wild' from the November 26th, 1986 edition of the *Chicago Tribune*.

'Stuck' contains an epigraph from an interview with Mae Noell, the owner of the roadside zoo where Lucy was born, in Dale Peterson and Jane Goodall's *Visions of Caliban: On Chimpanzees and People* (University of Georgia Press, 1993). The poem is also based on events detailed in Peterson and Goodall's book.

'Reunion Island' refers to a photo of Janis Carter and Lucy which can be found on Wikipedia: https://en.wikipedia.org/wiki/Lucy_(chimpanzee)

'For a Brief and Happy While' is based on information from Dale Peterson's *Chimpanzee Travels: On and Off the Road in Africa* (Addison-Wesley, 1995)

'Endings' is based on a discussion of the possible causes of Lucy's death in an article by Abuko Nature Reserve's Stella Brewer titled 'Did Poachers Really Kill Lucy the Sign Language Chimp?' from a November 2006 issue of *Animal People News*.

'Endings' reworks elements of the traditional English nursery rhyme 'Who Killed Cock Robin?'

'Obituaries' is based on details from the newspaper article 'Former OU Professor Dead at 64' from the February 4th, 1988 edition of *The Oklahoman*.

'Space Chimps (iii): Death of an Astronaut' is based on factual information from Colin Burgess and Chris Dubbs's *Animals in Space: From Research Rockets to the Space Shuttle* (Praxis, 2007).

'The Seven Primate Ages' is based on information from Ian Redmond's *The Primate Family Tree* (Firefly Books, 2008), which in turn references William Shakespeare's 'Ages of Man' speech from *As You Like It*.

Acknowledgments

I would like to thank my friend Stuart 'SBS' Barnes for the inexhaustible stream of insightful feedback and killer suggestions he sent my way during the slow writing of this book. Huge thanks also to Dani Corliss for reading so many of these poems in their earlier forms and for her generous encouragement. Thanks to Natasha Mitchell and Alice Allan for providing opportunities to share Lucy's story on the radio and in podcasts. Enormous gratitude must also go to Shane Strange and Recent Work Press for choosing to publish my collection of weird chimpanzee poems. Thanks to my family for always being there for me. Finally, love and endless appreciation to my wonderful partner Carlo for his cherished support.

An early version of 'Space Chimps (i): Property of Holloman Aerospace Medical' appeared in the June, 2017 issue of *Tincture*.

'Space Chimps (iii): Death of an Astronaut' was published in the Earth issue of *Cordite* in August, 2019.

About the Author

Benjamin Dodds is a Sydney-based poet who grew up in the NSW Riverina. He is the author of *Regulator*. His work appears in journals, anthologies and newspapers and has been broadcast on Radio National. He is a proud public school teacher. *Airplane Baby Banana Blanket* is his second book.

www.ingramcontent.com/pod-product-compliance
Lightning Source LLC
Chambersburg PA
CBHW020329010526
44107CB00054B/2031